Referee

Earning $50,000–$100,000 with a High School Diploma or Less

Announcer

Car Mechanic

Chef

Cosmetologist

DJ

Dog Groomer

Energizing Energy Markets:
Clean Coal, Shale, Oil, Wind, and Solar

Farming, Ranching, and Agriculture

Masseur & Massage Therapist

Personal Assistant

Presenting Yourself: Business Manners,
Personality, and Etiquette

Referee

The Arts: Dance, Music, Theater, and Fine Art

Truck Driver

Earning $50,000–$100,000
with a High School Diploma or Less

Referee

Marty Gitlin

Mason Crest

Mason Crest
450 Parkway Drive, Suite D
Broomall, PA 19008
www.masoncrest.com

Printed in the United States of America.

First printing
9 8 7 6 5 4 3 2 1

Series ISBN: 978-1-4222-2886-9
ISBN: 978-1-4222-2899-9
ebook ISBN: 978-1-4222-8935-8

The Library of Congress has cataloged the
        hardcopy format(s) as follows:

            Library of Congress Cataloging-in-Publication Data

Gitlin, Marty.
  Referee / Marty Gitlin.
    pages cm. – (Earning $50,000 - $100,000 with a high school diploma or less)
  Includes bibliographical references and index.
  ISBN 978-1-4222-2899-9 (hardcover) – ISBN 978-1-4222-2886-9 (series) – ISBN 978-1-4222-8935-8 (ebook)
  1. Sports–Vocational guidance–Juvenile literature. 2. Sports personnel–Employment–Juvenile literature. I. Title.
  GV734.3.G57 2014
  796.02'3–dc23
                                    2013011185
Produced by Vestal Creative Services.
www.vestalcreative.com

Contents

CHAPTER 1

Careers Without College

They work in front of thousands of people, but nobody comes to see *them*. They toil in the freezing cold or unbearable heat. They get no credit for making a hundred good decisions, but they are taunted and scorned for making one bad one.

Yet when they look at themselves in the mirror, they feel a great sense of accomplishment.

They are referees and umpires. No high school, college, or professional sporting event could be played without them. Their rulings on the baseball diamond, football field, or basketball court decide the outcome of any game.

Most professional sports officials work out of a suitcase. They travel all over the country during the season. They barely have time to say hello or goodbye to their families.

They work with other referees or umpires, but every call is their own. They must make split-second decisions in games played by athletes who are bigger, stronger, faster, and quicker than they are.

It is a lonely job. It is lonely in a near-empty stadium, but it is also lonely even in front of 50,000 or 100,000 fans

Firsthand Experience

Major League Baseball umpire Hunter Wendelstedt has known what it means to be an umpire since he was a child. He learned about the lifestyle and pressure of the job from his father Harry Wendelstedt. The elder Wendelstedt spent much of his time away from home as a National League umpire for thirty-two years. Hunter understood that it is a tough job, but he followed in his father's footsteps.

Times have changed for umpires since Harry first stepped on a Major League field in 1966. Every game is now on a national television broadcast. Every close call Wendelstedt makes is examined. He knows he must give his best effort both in front of a huge crowd or a small gathering.

"Sure, it's fun working a sellout at Yankee Stadium [in New York City] during a pennant race," Wendelstedt said. "But you get in trouble as an ump when you think you can come down to a place like Tampa and take a night off. That's when you'll be a step out of position for a call—and *SportsCenter* [on ESPN] will show you missing one [in Tampa] as they will if you do it in New York.

"Your friends think it's funny when they see you on TV because of a call. But they're the same people who, in their job, if … they have a bad day at the office, will pout for three days. They couldn't imagine getting a call from one of their friends saying, 'Hey, I heard you really [stunk] at work yesterday!'"

Wendelstedt attended college for two years, but he didn't need a college education to become a Major League umpire. No major sports leagues require their officials to be college educated.

Careers Without College

A college classroom can bring knowledge and wisdom to any young person, but other life experiences can do the same. Some young adults prefer to take a direct approach to the pursuit of a career through other forms of training instead of college.

The Bureau of Labor Statistics lists forty high-paying professions that do not require college educations, including those involved with aviation, construction, police work, electronics, firefighting, dental hygiene, nursing, fashion design, and farming. A desire to enter one of these fields should top the list of reasons not to attend college. **Passion** should be the primary reason to pursue any profession. People rarely perform well in a job they do not enjoy.

What Does It Take to Be an Umpire?

Officiating at sports events is certainly not a boring job! Referees and umpires in such sports as basketball, football, and baseball are in an action-packed setting. They play **critical** roles in any event. All eyes are upon them when they make a call that can affect the outcome of a game. Refs and umps enjoy the excitement, but they cannot allow it to affect their concentration. Officials must remain focused on the task at hand at all times.

Not everybody is born with the personality traits needed to **thrive** in such an environment. But those who don't have all the right traits can still work on improving those skills. If you get your feelings hurt too easily or you can't control your temper, you may not be cut out to be a sport official—after all, criticism from athletes and the media is part of the job. Every **veteran** official has been screamed at by players, condemned by sportswriters and broadcasters, and booed unmercifully by thousands of fans. Some have been pushed by athletes on the field or court.

Umpires and referees must show restraint and **exude** confidence that they are making the right call in the face of verbal and even physical **confrontation**. They can on occasion throw a coach or player from a game if the abuse warrants such action—but there is nothing they can do about jeering from fans and the media.

Technology and sports leagues have provided greater aid to officials in recent years. The use of instant replay on certain types of plays has allowed them to re-examine their calls and change them if incorrect. That has taken some of the pressure off them, but officiating remains one of the most closely **scrutinized** professions in the United States.

Instant replay has highlighted the fact that referees and umpires are only human and can make mistakes.

Patience is another virtue for anyone pursuing a career in sports officiating. Refs and umps follow the same path as the athletes; both must work hard to improve their skills at the lower levels before moving up. Only the best are promoted to Major League Baseball, the National Football League, or the National Basketball Association. Some individuals might become upset over the need to polish their crafts in the minor leagues or high school and smaller college sports for less pay. Such impatience leads to poorer job performance and a smaller chance to reach the big leagues.

Some people think that psychological skills such as concentration, confidence, and staying calm under pressure are skills you have to be born with. That is simply not true. These qualities are talents that can be practiced and improved. Only those who are open to developing psychological skills necessary to become an effective official can advance to the highest levels.

Looking at the Words

Critical roles are very important.

If you **thrive**, you do well and grow strong.

Someone who is a **veteran** has experience doing something.

When you **exude** something, it flows out of you so that everyone can see it.

A **confrontation** is when two sides meet in a disagreement.

Something that is **scrutinized** is looked at very closely.

Long-time NFL referee Dick McKenzie understands that succeeding in his field required as many mental and emotional skills as physical ones. His list of such attributes is a long one. "You have to be **decisive**, coachable, and have **impeccable integrity**," he said. "You need the ability to concentrate and stay focused. It's important to accept criticism, learn from mistakes, and not take yourself too seriously. You have to show consistent good judgment and communicate, as well as an ability to function as part of a team."

Athletes have coaches they can turn to for guidance, while officials must also seek out **mentors** who are more experienced and accomplished. They cannot be too proud to accept advice!

Mountain West Conference referee coordinator Ken Rivera believes being humble is an essential personality trait for young officials. "If [an official wants] to advance or even get better at their current level, then they need to find that person who's working at the top," he said. "Humble yourself and go to that person and say, 'Hey, I want to be where you are. What are some things that you've done to make yourself successful to get there and, knowing my personality traits, my officiating style, what are some things that I can do to improve myself?'"

A keen interest in sports certainly makes it easier for young adults who want to become professional or major college refs or umps. Those

who have played a particular sport and understand its rules are the best candidates for success as officials.

The physical tasks involved with sports officiating can also be challenging, especially in sports that require a lot of movement. Baseball umpires are often less fit because quickness and speed are not major requirements in their job, but basketball and football referees must be in excellent shape. They run up and down the court or field to stay in position to make correct calls. The same holds true for other sports such as soccer and lacrosse. Any ref or ump who wants to make the most of her potential will need to exercise and eat properly.

Becoming a sports official at the highest level doesn't take a college degree. But it does take motivation and a willingness to learn!

CHAPTER 2

What Do Umps and Referees Do?

Fans head to sports arenas and stadiums all around America to watch their favorite teams play. The media also streams in to analyze the game.

For a few hours, the officials are under a microscope. They are judged by the amount of attention they receive. If they go unnoticed, that means nobody has questioned their calls. If they become the center of an argument, an athlete or an entire team has gotten angry with their decision. They prefer to be **anonymous**!

Very few people care that the quality of an ump's work is determined not by what he does during

games, but rather how well he prepares for his job on a daily basis. Few people care about the years of training that molded a ref's careers . . . or about her personal life or the strain of travel that keeps her from her family for days or even weeks at a time. All fans and the media want to see is a well-officiated game. The life of an umpire or referee is one of the great unknowns of American sport. Very few people know the hours of work and details that fill an ump's schedule every week.

Firsthand Experience

Bill Carollo served as an NFL referee for twenty years before retiring in 2009. He later managed officials in four major college football conferences. He knows as well as anyone that the tasks of NFL referees do not end when they trudge off the field after a game. Carollo explained that the chores for the week begin on Sunday night, just hours after the chores from the previous week conclude.

"We would actually go back to the hotel [on Sunday nights], have food brought in and look at the TV tape of [the game]," Carollo explained. ". . .There will be a brief review of all the penalties, any controversial plays. As a referee, I have to send in multiple reports to the league about the fouls [and] about anything that happened on the sideline or anything unusual in the game."

Like most NFL referees, Carollo had a side job. He did not simply travel around the country to officiate football games. His other work

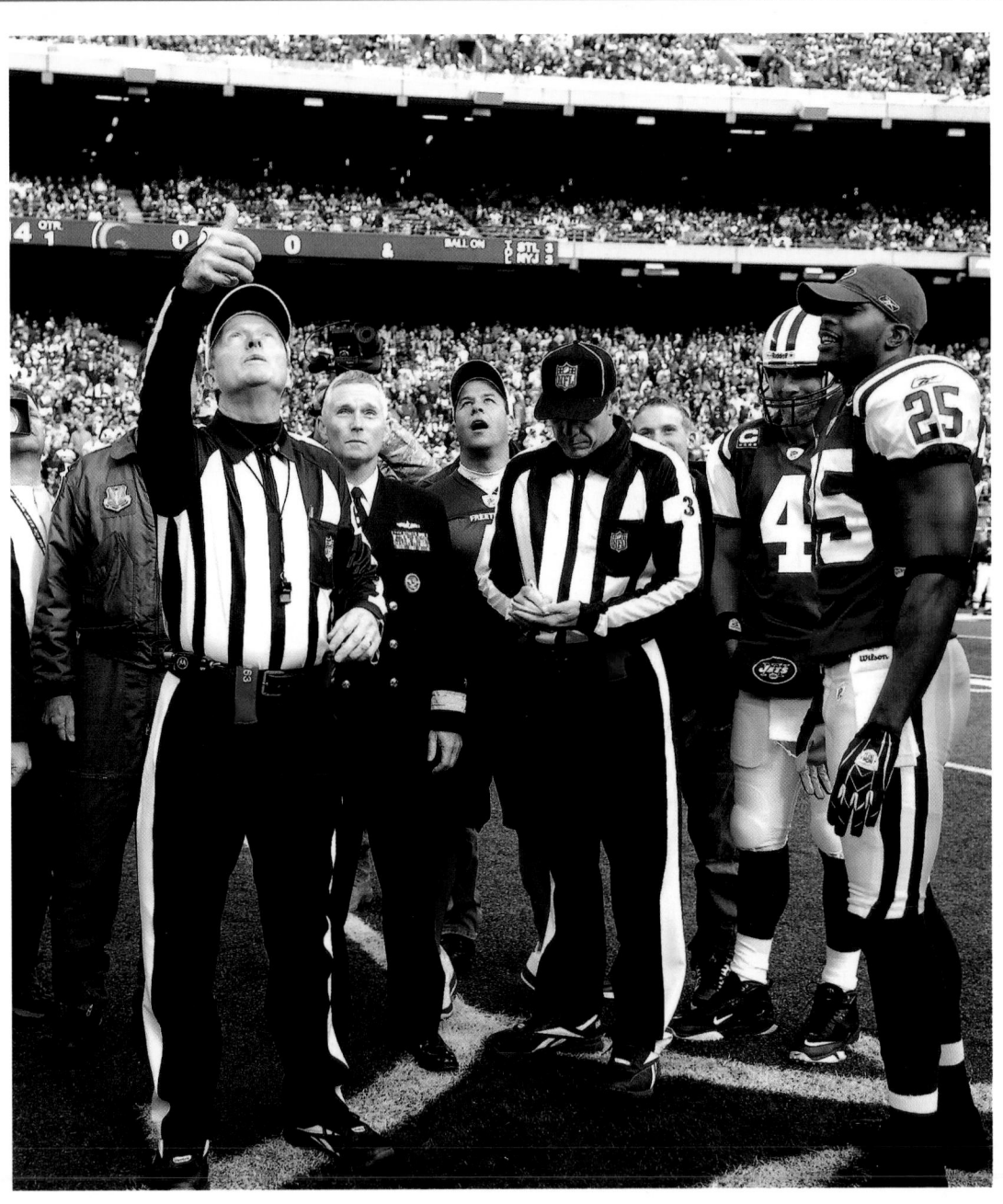

Here Bill Carollo is doing the coin toss before a game between the New York Jets and the St. Louis Rams in 2008.

What Do Umps and Referees Do?

required spending considerable time in Europe, South America, and Asia. He often jetted to other countries of the world on Monday, but took time off to participate in a conference call with the NFL front office.

"A lot of times I would work a ballgame, fly to Beijing," he explained. "And then the phone would ring. 'I'm looking for you. There were a couple of offside calls [we'd like to go over]. Where are you?' I said, 'I'm checking into my hotel in China.'"

Carollo had little time to unwind once he returned home. While he was overseas, his performance the previous Sunday was being graded and sent back to him in a report by a former referee. He studied it with the man who graded it before preparing for the next game. He and his team of officials examined the habits of the two teams scheduled to play that Sunday to gain an idea of what to expect from them. Carollo and his teammates also took a written quiz every week about NFL rules.

The referees fly to their game sites on Friday night or Saturday morning. They must be in their cities within twenty-four hours of Sunday kickoff. They meet with their fellow crewmembers to prepare for the game and watch a video prepared by the league. It features about twenty-five plays on which referees made mistakes from games played throughout the NFL the previous week.

The toughest, but must enjoyable assignment was yet to come for Corolla, though: the game itself. "That's the best part of the week," he said. "Sunday afternoon at kickoff, those three hours, it's beautiful. There's pressure and we'll screw up calls and we'll make some mistakes, but solving those problems and sorting through those difficult calls are why we do it. Just to see how good we really are, so that's really what we work for . . . because it's the hardest thing that most of us have ever tried to do."

Sports officials who use their brains and concentrate make fewer errors. Each major sport requires a different set of additional skills for its officials that sometimes mirror those of its athletes.

Basketball Officials and Football Referees

Basketball is played on the smallest surface of the three major sports. The game features quick passes and body movements, as well as frequent contact. NBA players are considered the most athletic in American sport. Those who officiate their games must also be athletic enough to keep up with the action. Running up and down the floor for forty-eight minutes in an indoor arena tests their **stamina**. A keen eye and sharp focus are necessary for basketball officials to call the sport correctly.

College football and NFL referees also work under great physical strain. Unlike NBA officials, they must deal with weather conditions in games that are about an hour longer. Games in August can be unbearably hot. Games in December and January in northern cities can be freezing cold. Every football official is responsible for different zones on the field. The referee, umpire, head linesman, line judge, field judge, side judge, and back judge are scattered across the playing field. They call penalties against players or determine possession of the ball on the areas of the playing surface for which they are in charge.

Calls required from basketball and football officials are often **subjective**. When two or more players collide or attempt to control the ball, there may be no black-and-

> ## Looking at the Words
>
> **Stamina** is the ability to keep exercising for long periods of time.
>
> Something that is **subjective** is influenced by personal tastes and opinions rather than hard facts.

During his time as the manager of the Baltimore Orioles, Earl Weaver was famous for giving umpires a hard time.

white answer as to who was in the wrong. But the officials must be decisive. They must make a quick decision based on what they saw.

Baseball Umpires

The same holds true for baseball umpires, though physical requirements are far less demanding for them. Overweight umpires are far more common than out-of-shape basketball or football officials. Being an umpire doesn't demand all that much exercise—but the mental strain can be intense. At least one of the four baseball umpires makes a call on every play. A home-plate umpire barks out each ball and strike call, and the base umpires determine if a runner is safe or out. Concentration and a keen eye are required on close pitches, or when there is only a split-second difference between the arrival of the ball and the runner.

A Difficult Manager

Among the most argumentative managers was Earl Weaver, who guided the Baltimore Orioles to four American League pennants in the 1960s and 1970s. Umpire Larry Barnett was often forced into face-to-face quarrels with Weaver. "He's goofy," Barnett said in 1979. "He can't control himself—ranting, raving, and screaming. Every time he comes out of the dugout, it's as if he's shot from a cannon."

Umpires discuss a play at a game between the Colorado Rockies and the Houston Astros.

Baseball umpires often do their job in the spotlight. That's because fans and cameras in their sport focus on individual players. One player pitches the ball, one player hits the ball, one player fields the ball, and one player catches the ball. The same is true for umpires. When the camera catches them making a mistake, they have nowhere to hide. The slow pace of baseball gives fans time to boo umpires when they think the umpires made a bad call. It also lets players and managers race onto the field and get into long, spirited arguments with the umpires who often have to throw them out of the game. Umpires have been on the front line against angry players and managers since the sport was organized nearly one hundred and fifty years ago. Officials have always been required to enforce the rules of any sport. They have been as much a part of the game over the years as the players. In fact, verbal battles between umpires and players or managers are a time-honored baseball tradition. They add to the entertainment value of the game.

Careers as Sports Officials

As the sports have grown, so have the requirements for their officials. Athletes in all sports have grown faster, quicker, and stronger due to advancements in training and the lure of far bigger salaries. The pace of the action on the field and court has become faster and more difficult to officiate. Referees in sports that require the most athleticism, such as football and basketball, must be sharper than ever before. Thanks to the growth of the sports world, there are also more jobs than ever before as well.

Up until 1961, Major League Baseball had just sixteen teams, eight each in the American League and National League. Two more teams were added in both leagues in 1969. Since then, new franchises have been awarded to cities across the country, giving Major League

A good way to get your foot in the door if you want to be a volleyball referee might be to volunteer as a line judge. Line judges decide whether balls are in or out, and they signal when a ball crosses the net outside the crossing space and when a server footfaults. They also authorize game interruptions, substitutions, and time-outs.

Baseball a total of thirty teams. More teams translates to more games played—and more umpires required.

The same holds true for the NFL, NBA, and National Hockey League. The NFL boasted twelve teams in 1959 and thirty-two in 2012. The NBA has evolved from nine teams in 1966 to thirty in 2012. The NHL had a mere six teams in 1967 and thirty in 2012. More teams equals more games . . . equals more sports officials needed.

The growing popularity of other sports such as soccer and lacrosse in the last few decades has provided still more opportunities for officials. So have major women's college sports such as softball, basketball, and volleyball. The explosion of participation in various girls' high school sports has resulted in a higher number of jobs for officials at that level. It has allowed more referee and umpiring prospects to receive training, but has also resulted in greater competition for college and professional sports jobs.

Becoming a sports official is an exciting career path. It doesn't require a college education—but it does require hard work.

CHAPTER 3

How Can I Become a Sports Official?

The journey is different for every referee in every sport. Many officials who have earned their way into professional leagues started out with only a high school diploma and experience in community or recreational competition. For many sports officials, their career journeys stop at the high school or small college level. That is where many officials are content to remain. The best and most ambitious officials, however, will go on to major college or professional games.

The path to success is different for every official fortunate enough to reach the NFL or NBA or Major League Baseball.

It requires a mix of luck, skill, and aggressiveness to achieve the ultimate goal. Some refs and umps land in the big leagues soon after their career voyage begins. It takes others decades to work their way to the top.

Football

According to the website Refstripes.com, today, there is a shortage of football officials all over the country. However, officiating is a very demanding career.

First, you must be physically fit. Football refs are constantly moving—and they must do so in all kinds of weather, from sweltering heat to icy rain. You also need to be emotionally fit. In other words, you must be able to take criticism without getting upset. You must be able to stay calm under pressure.

If you think you have what it takes, your first step is to find your local football referee association. Get in touch with officials in your area. Get to know them. Ask their advice. As with many other jobs, **networking** is important. The more people you know, the easier it is to get started, because when openings come up, your name will come to mind.

Next, you might want to find an older or experienced official to be your mentor. A wealth of knowledge can be gained by talking with an official who has been through the ranks. He or she can teach you the ins and outs of officiating. If you don't know any officials, go to a game and ask the crew working the game for some contact information. Or you might ask an administrator at your local high school.

You don't need to go to college—but you will need to work hard for years at a time. Still, football officials think it's well worth it. According to Walt Coleman, an NFL referee, "The opportunity to stand on the sideline before a game and hear the National Anthem still gives me goose bumps. To be a part of the great game of football and work with tremendous people will always be a thrill. We are the integrity of the game which brings with it huge responsibility." Rogers Redding,

another referee, says, "Football officiating is a terrific **avocation**; it combines doing something that is hard and tremendous fun at the same time."

When asked how to rise through the ranks as a referee, Redding says, "First and foremost you had better be the best official you can be at the level you are currently working—that means you involve yourself with your local association—attend meetings, clinics, work all of the games that your work and family schedule will allow."

So how can you hope to be one of the lucky few who will make a living reffing for the NFL? The NFL lists a number of steps a ref needs to take before he can blow his whistle in one of its games. Refs must participate in the Football Officiating Academy, learn at various clinics, gain experience at the community and high school levels, and pass tests of knowledge. Five years of officiating experience is also required. The NFL sends scouts to college games to grade officials for possible promotion. They are looking for officials with character, knowledge of the rules, athleticism, decisiveness, and strong field presence.

Many NFL officials receive exposure and experience at lower-level professional leagues, such as the Canadian Football League, Arena Football League, and various indoor football leagues. Some are invited to work in training camps for NFL teams. The best are then interviewed for job openings—and if they're good enough, they're hired.

Baseball

The website Educational Portal offers four steps to follow in order to become a baseball umpire.

First of all, learn the game. If you want to be an ump, you'll need to learn as much as you can about the rules and regulations of baseball. Study the various baseball handbooks, including those offered by the Little League, National Collegiate Athletic Association (NCAA) and Major League Baseball (MLB). Watch baseball on television. Attend games. Play baseball! Make sure the rules and actions are ingrained into your mind!

Success Tip

Get to know umpires. This is a great way to network and learn about the job. Ask these umpires questions about the game and about umpire associations.

Your second step? Make sure you have the physical and psychological strength to do the job. Umpires need to be able to stand or bend for extended periods of time. They need to be able to work in all kinds of weather, including high temperatures. Major League umpires also have to have 20/20 vision, with or without corrective lenses. They need to have the ability to make sound judgments. Most of all, umpires must be able to communicate clearly. They need to be able to cope with stress. This requires a lot of self-confidence and emotional stability.

If you've made it this far, the third step is to attend an umpire training program. Even umpiring at the amateur level—such as Little League, high school, and college—requires some training. You may be able to attend a three-day umpire clinic. There are also umpiring schools, such as The Umpire School and Jim Evans Academy of Professional Umpiring, that prepare people for professional baseball careers (and those not interested in professional baseball can also attend). In order to complete the program, you'll need to pass both a written exam and an evaluation period. Once you have, you'll be qualified to move into minor league umpiring—which is what you'll need to do before you can hope to work in the Major League.

But there's a fourth step as well: certification. Local or regional baseball umpire associations offer this. You'll need to pass a written exam

made up of questions related to the rules and regulations of umpiring. To maintain certification, baseball umpires are required to attend yearly clinics and field sessions to stay updated on changes in the game.

Basketball

Education Portal also explains the steps you'll need to take if it's basketball reffing that interests you. First, you'll need to find and join the local basketball officials association. These groups meet regularly, offer trainings, and help new referees gain officiating experience on court.

Success Tip

Get in touch with high school athletic directions, association assigners, and other officials. If you can make friends with these people, they can help you get games and gain experience. You'll also need to attend local officiating camps and clinics. Once you have obtained a level of knowledge and experience at the high school level, you'll be able to move up the ladder to college-level officiating.

You'll need to start in the peewee or junior leagues to get needed experience. After that, you can move up to high school reffing. You can't hope to move up to college reffing until you have more than a year of youth league experience. This is an unspoken rule.

College basketball is very competitive, for referees as well as athletes. Officials wanting to work at the college level will have to enter a college conference and work those games. You'll need to contact college athletic directors or sports information directors for help in

getting into working college level basketball games. It's a good idea to become linked with the National Association of Intercollegiate Athletics (NAIA) or the National Collegiate Athletic Association (NCAA) Division III conference. As you get great experience in Division III or the NAIA, you'll be able to move up in divisions. Meanwhile,

Looking at the Words

A **résumé** is one or two pages that list all of your work experiences and credentials.

keep attending more camps in order to improve your officiating skills. Attending these camps and clinics will also help you get to know conference commissions and supervisors who assign games. Network! You also should consider officiating for minor leagues. Sometimes, the NBA will select referees from the college level and minor league officials.

The highest level you can hope to reach as basketball referee is to officiate for the NBA and WNBA. You'll need to contact the National Basketball Association's office, which will tell you the steps to take. You will be required to complete an application and provide a **résumé**. Then, if the NBA is interested, you will be invited to a summer identification camp. Here, each potential ref will have the chance to officiate. They'll also get to know the professional staff. After the summer identification camp, if you've been successful, you will be placed in a development program, which will include in-season as well as off-season camps. People will be watching your development. If you do well, you will be hired to work in the National Basketball Development League (NBDL). There, you will gain experience officiating for NBDL, WNBA, and NBA games. If you're successful, you will become a regular member of the NBA or WNBA staff.

What All Sports Officials Need

The paths created for officials by professional sports leagues are indeed all different. But they all require similar physical, mental, and emotional traits. The Bureau of Labor Statistics lists these five traits as necessary for any ref or ump:

1. **Communication skills:** Umpires, referees, and other sports officials must have good communication skills because they instruct athletes and settle disputes between competing players. Some sports officials also must communicate **violations** to opposing team players, coaches, and spectators.
2. **Decision-making skills:** Umpires, referees, and other sports officials must judge various situations and often make split-second decisions.
3. **Good vision:** Umpires, referees, and other sports officials must have good vision in order to see exactly what is happening.
4. **Stamina:** Because many umpires, referees, and sports officials are required to stand, walk, run, or squat for long periods, having stamina is important.
5. **Teamwork:** Because many umpires, referees, and sports officials work in teams, the ability to cooperate and come to a mutual decision is essential.

Looking at the Words

Violations are situations where rules are broken.

If you have all five of these traits, you may have what it takes to earn a living as a ref or ump. But the difference in pay and prestige between the lower levels and the top is significant—and there are no guarantees that you'll make it to the top.

It's Not Easy!

Major League Baseball umpire Sam Holbrook explained, "Once you're in Double-A and Triple-A, that's when you're wondering: Am I going to make it? Is it worth it? Because nothing is guaranteed. You have some dark times. Even the actual umpiring can be tougher; the players aren't as good and everyone is hungry, clawing. You're more likely to get into [an argument] with a player or coach in the minors."

About forty of the three hundred students—about 13 percent—that enroll each year in umpire schools are placed into the minor leagues, and only about 2 percent of them will work Major League Baseball games. The most difficult jump is to the professional ranks. There are just sixty-eight umpires in Major League Baseball, eighty-five officials in the NBA, and 121 in the NFL. Openings usually occur when someone re-tires, and the competition then is fierce. Some umps and refs who make it to the top must hone their craft for decades. Others are lucky and talented enough to advance to the highest level in a much shorter time frame.

Barry Mano knows all about the difficulty of rising to the top. He is the founder of the National Association of Sports Officials and a former major college basketball referee. "You have 121 [NFL officials] right now," he said. "You have on the order of 70,000 football officials work-ing high school and above."

Dick McKenzie toiled as an NFL referee for nearly twenty years be-fore he had the chance to blow his first whistle in that league. He served

Scouting for Umps

Major League Baseball has started scouting for umpires the same way it does for players. Umpire scouts find potential MLB umpires at one-day camps around the country and from the military. Then they send boys who show promise to a week-long umpire training program at the Urban Youth Academy in Compton California. From there, the best candidates will go to a five-week training course.

Malachi Moore is an umpire who made it through the program and now works to recruit new umpires for the academy. He says, "It's definitely an unlimited ceiling. The guys catch on and they catch on quick. They don't know much about the profession going in, but once they get a little taste of the Compton camp, they figure it out quick and they want to do it. I'm there to explain things to them, and so are these veteran guys. When the veteran guys come, we all just sit back and listen."

Darrell Miller, MLB's vice president of youth and facility development, says he's working to create "Major League citizens" who have a chance at going on to greater education and opportunity. That could mean scouting, coaching, or umpiring, but it could also mean a job outside the sporting world. Miller, a former MLB catcher, wants to let boys know that they can be anything they want to be.

as a high school referee from 1963 to 1976, and worked small college games for six seasons during that period. He was finally hired by the NFL in 1978 and eventually officiated four conference championship games and two Super Bowls.

Joey Crawford took a much speedier route to becoming one of the premier officials in the NBA. His willingness to gain a lot of experience from the start helped him reach his goal at a younger age. "I started right at the bottom, did thirteen games in the first week that I started reffing in local leagues," he recalled. "I went from gym to gym, didn't know what I was doing. I was eighteen, didn't even have a car. I worked my way up. Then I got into the old Eastern League, and I worked in the Eastern League for four years. I got into the NBA when I was twenty-five."

Mano, McKenzie, and Crawford know that there is no substitute for game experience. But they also understand the value and necessity of training. Professional leagues understand it as well, which is why they require their officials to attend training schools. These aren't college; they're much shorter and much less expensive. If you want to be an umpire, though, you should expect to plunk down about $3400 for one of two five-week courses sponsored by Major League Baseball. Only those with a high school diploma and proven 20/20 vision, who are in good physical condition, can enroll. And only the best graduates get the chance to umpire in even the lowest of the minor leagues. Umpires must spend at least one season in Rookie League baseball and six more in the minors to get a shot at the majors. An average of just two or three positions opens up in the big leagues every year.

If you want to be a sports official, you'll also have to accept odd working hours. Most workers go to work on weekdays from around 8 a.m. to 5 p.m. But high schools, college conferences, and professional sports leagues want games played when people are free to watch them — so sports officials have to work during the hours when other people

Was the runner's foot touching the plate before the baseman caught the ball? Umpires have to be able to observe closely in order to make accurate calls.

don't. High school football games are usually played on Friday nights. College football games most often occur on Saturday afternoons. NFL teams compete on Sunday afternoons and nights, as well as Monday and Thursday nights. Baseball games take place at night and on Sunday afternoons. NBA teams play almost always at night.

You'll also have to work many hours outside of game situations. Officials prepare for every game. They need to keep up with rules changing, stay in contact with the league office and various heads of officials, and make certain they're on the same page with their fellow referees and umpires.

Veteran NFL referee Ed Hochuli even practices looking confident in front of his mirror before each game. "I think the appearance we portray as referees [is] very important," he said. "When you say something, you don't want to be stumbling over your words. I've got a box full of play situations. I'll go over the announcements that need to be made and do the announcements, so when it comes up in games, I say it smoothly and not come out looking like an idiot."

All officials come out looking like an idiot when they blow a call on occasion. They make no more mistakes than the average person on the job—but the errors made by most workers are not televised coast-to-coast or witnessed live by eighty thousand sometimes-hostile people.

Considering the abuse they must often handle, officials deserve to be well paid! They don't have college degrees—but they have each worked hard to get where they are.

CHAPTER 4

How Much Can I Make?

When and where are people who make nearly $10,000 a week surrounded by others who earn as much as a hundred times that? The answer: Each Sunday from September through January at every NFL stadium in the country.

High-Level Earnings

The most experienced NFL referees receive a weekly check of almost $10,000. That sounds pretty good—and it is! Yet the salaries of every

player on the field are far higher. But the thousands of fans at the games and watching on TV are there to see the athletes perform, not the officials.

Still, the most experienced football referees at the major college and professional levels have above-average salaries. They are represented by unions that bargain with the leagues for the highest salaries possible. NFL officials finally settled a bitter contract disagreement in 2012 that netted an eight-year agreement, which will give officials an average annual salary of $173,000 in 2013 and $205,000 by 2019.

Those figures compare well to the money earned by Major League Baseball umpires and NBA referees. Some people think that NFL officials should not earn as much as umpires and NBA refs, however, because NFL refs only work one game a week, while baseball umpires toil on the field nearly every night from April through September, and their NBA peers officiate several games a week. However, officials in all sports spend hours a day in preparation. In addition, the NFL earns far more money in national television contracts than their baseball and basketball counterparts do. Football officials believe they deserve a piece of that pie.

Moonlighting

Many NFL refs have side jobs as well. Mike Carey, for example, holds eight patents for snow sports apparel. Walt Coleman is a dairy farmer. Jeff Triplette fought with the Army Reserve during the Persian Gulf War and was awarded a bronze star. Gene Steratore doubles as a college basketball official and has worked March Madness, the exciting season-ending tournament. Ed Hochuli is a lawyer.

The starting salary for a Major League Baseball umpire is around $120,000. The most experienced can earn an annual salary as high as $350,000—and they don't even work twelve months a year! Their seasons begin during spring training in late February, and they often work into the playoffs and World Series, which concludes at the end of October. Top umpires get less than four months off. Baseball umpires also receive $340 a day for hotel, food, rental car, and other expenses. Umpires spend nearly all their time on the road and the costs add up.

While baseball umpires arrive in a town and stay for three to four days to work a series of games between two teams, NBA referees bounce from one city to another. They often fly into town one day and leave that night. Their schedules are more hectic than those of other sports officials. So it's no wonder that NBA referees are paid well. Their annual are between $100,000 and $550,000. They usually officiate at as many as a hundred games a year, including the preseason, regular season, and postseason.

Earnings at Lower-Level Officiating

The difference in earnings between professional sports officials and those at the lower levels is huge, however. Very few high school and college umpires and referees can make a living without holding down side jobs. Only the college basketball referees in greatest demand can earn enough money to consider the work full-time.

National Collegiate Athletic Association (NCAA) Coordinator of Men's Basketball Officiating, John Adams, explained that the top six to eight officials in college basketball earn as much as $2,500 to $3,000 a game, but they must pay their own travel costs and other expenses out of

Refs at high school basketball games have a chance to earn some extra money and gain experience.

that money. They must also cover their own health insurance. He added that only about forty NCAA basketball referees earned enough money in 2009 to see their jobs as a full-time career.

As a beginning referee, you need to know what to expect. First of all you can't expect to earn a living from reffing, at least not at first. You're unlikely to get a full schedule until after you have some experience. Some states require refs to work on a chain crew for a year or two before moving up to be an official. Once you are an official, even then you'll likely be expected to start at the lower levels and work your way up through the divisions. First-year football officials can't work playoff games. The amount of experience required varies between states and associations, but usually, you'll need to work four to ten years and a certain number of varsity games before you'll be able to work a playoff game. So don't expect to get rich as a football official! If you're very committed and willing to work hard, you may be able to rise up through the ranks—but the average pay for a junior varsity game is between $45 and $70, and the average for a senior varsity game is between $65 and $100. According to the Bureau of Labor Statistics (BLS), in 2010, the average yearly income for sports officials was only $22,800. High school football refs often say, "We don't do it for the money!"

But amateur sports do offer a wide variety of opportunities. High school and college sports that require game officials include gymnastics, soccer, swimming, hockey, softball, volleyball, track and field, and lacrosse. Those sports provide experience and money ambitious officials often use to attend officiating schools.

Sports officials at the top 10 percent, earn more than $50,000, however. Here's the bottom line if you want to be an ump or a ref: How motivated are you? If you're willing to put in the time and effort to reach the major college or professional ranks, you could end up with a high-paying job. Or you might want to look at officiating as your hobby instead, a good way to have fun and make some extra money.

To help you make up your mind, it's a good idea to understand what the years ahead are expected to hold for the field of sports officiating.

How Much Can I Make?

CHAPTER 5

What's the Future of Sports Officials?

Nobody has a crystal ball that can predict with certainty the future of sports officiating. But trends over the last few decades offer hints about the greatest opportunities for those seeking to advance in the field. The BLS reports that the number of jobs is expected to increase, with officials' average wages also increasing by 20 percent over the next ten years.

In 2012, Shannon Eastin was the first woman to officiate at an NFL game. Her advice to girls who are dreaming of following in her footsteps: "You have to work harder, and do everything in your power to control what you can. You never know who's watching."

The Outlook for Women

Women's sports at all levels are expected to grow. The number of recreational leagues for girls will increase in a wide variety of sports, and more high schools and colleges will offer women's sports programs. This will mean more jobs for refs and umps. However, men's college teams make more money because they are televised and have more fans—which also means their officials can earn more than women's teams' officials do.

But if you're a young women who dreams of officiating in men's professional sports, there's good news: no rules stand in your way. Although Major League Baseball and the NHL have never had a woman official up through 2012, female umpires have reached the minor league baseball level, and the NFL and NBA are starting to open their doors to women officals. The fact that such leagues are open to women suggests that more will join the ranks in the future.

Officiating at the Olympics

Olympic sports also require sports officials. Every two years, judges and referees are needed for Winter Olympic sports for both men and women, including skiing, figure skating, and hockey, and for Summer Olympic sports, such as volleyball and gymnastics. Those jobs are scarce, however, and the process to gain certification is long and difficult.

The Future for MLB Umpires

Rich Rieker, the director of umpire development for Major League Baseball, says he's thrilled that the MLB is seeking new umpires, and he's hopeful about the future of umping. "It's a great profession," said Rieker, who's a former big-league umpire. "And we're giving even more people the opportunity."

Rieker, who knows firsthand, says it's the greatest job in the world. "It is arduous, but the dividends at the end are worth it," he says.

He also says it takes time before you can expect to make a living as an umpire in the big leagues. "Normally, after your sixth or seventh year, if you're working with us, you're going to get some games on a replacement basis based on injuries and vacations for Major League umpires. When you're finally hired, it may take up to ten years, but at the end of the day you're going to get a taste of that big league stuff in Spring Training after about six or seven years. Now, it may seem like a long time—and it definitely is—but it's worth it in the end."

Global Sports

The NBA, NFL, and Major League Baseball may need more referees and umpires as they grow internationally. The three primary leagues are unlikely to add more than a few American teams, since nearly all the major cities already have franchises, but the leagues may spread into Europe and Mexico. The NFL attempted to move into other countries cities by promoting a separate league called NFL Europe. Although it wasn't successful, NFL officials have still voiced an interest in adding franchises on the other side of the Atlantic Ocean. The NBA and Major League Baseball have also looked into placing teams outside of the United States and Canada. If this does become a reality, so will the need for additional officials. These officials could expect to earn good salaries—while having the chance to see the world! But who knows when or if this will happen.

Good News and Bad

For those sports officials working at lower levels, the future is equally hard to predict. On the one hand, as the population grows alongside an emphasis on physical fitness, organized sports are likely to thrive. At the same time, however, many schools are facing budget problems that could mean they will have to cut their athletic programs.

The BLS predicts:

> Overall job prospects for umpires, referees, and sports officials are expected to be good. Job opportunities should be best for people seeking part-time . . . jobs at the high school level. Officials

NEW YORK POST

Page Six®

LATE CITY FINAL

OH SAY CAN'T YOU SEE?

Post photo composite

SEE SPORTS

Blind refs ruining America's game

This cover of the *New York Post* is a good example of the anger and criticism sports officials often face.

in women's sports may have better job opportunities and face less competition for jobs. Competition is expected for higher-paying jobs at the college level and will be even greater for jobs in professional sports.

The increased use of instant replay also seems inevitable. Players, fans, coaches, and the media demand that officials get calls right, even if they must be reversed. Some people are worried that better technology could result in the replacement of referees or umpires with computerized officiating. For instance, some believe that balls and strikes and close plays on the bases in a baseball game can be more accurately judged through technology.

The good news for those who yearn to advance in the field is that no sports league seems to be considering replacing officials with any form of instant replay. Those running the leagues have stressed that human error is as much a part of officiating as mistakes made by athletes in their performances. As long as there are sports, there will be a need for officials.

But if you want to be a sports official, there are no short cuts. This was confirmed in 2012 during a labor dispute between the NFL and its officials. The NFL decided to use replacement referees from the high school and small college ranks—but the decision proved to be a disaster. Several poor calls on the field brought the wrath of fans and players. Former veteran NFL referee Dick McKenzie explained why. He also spoke about the future of the field and why former players will not provide competition for referees in that league. "NFL officiating is not easy, as was proven by the 'displacement' officials."

After all, refs and umps are noticed only when they make a mistake. They are booed and criticized; they have to keep their composure

A top tennis umpire can expect to earn $80,000 to 96,000 a year, but it takes a long time to get there! Most earn around $48,000; a line judge can expect to earn $32,000.

The Future for NFL Refs

Based on a contract between the NFL and the NFL Referee Association signed in September 2012, NFL referees will earn an average of $173,000 in 2013, and move up to an average of $205,000 by 2019.

A plan to introduce a new group of developmental officials was also approved as part of the contract. These developmental officials will work with current NFL refs to develop their skills. The developmental officials will not be NFLRA members and cannot work games until they are graded high enough to join the ranks of regular NFL officials.

under intense pressure. Most of them will never earn enough money to be rich—and yet most of them love what they do.

If you're one of the lucky ones who rise to the top of this field, you won't get there by going to college. Experience, hard work, and motivation will be your keys to success.

Find Out More

In Books

Boga, Steve. *How to Umpire Baseball and Softball: An Introduction to Basic Umpiring Skills*. New York: CreateSpace, 2009.

Caminsky, Jeffrey. *The Referee's Survival Guide*. Livonia, Mich.: New Alexandria Press, 2007.

Fehler, Gene. *Never Blame the Umpire*. Grand Rapids, Mich.: Zonderkidz, 2011.

Finn, Ron. *On the Lines: The Adventures of a Linesman in the NHL*. Ontario, Canada: Rubicon Publishing, 2002.

Fitzgerald, Mike. *Third Man in the Ring: 33 of Boxing's Best Referees and Their Stories*. Dulle, Va.: Potomac Books, 2013.

Kratz, Marilyn. *Umpire in a Skirt: The Amanda Clement Story*. Pierre: South Dakota State Historical Society, 2011.

Martin, Billy; Tim Malloy; and Alan Battista. *Beyond the Rules—Basketball Officiating Volume 1: Techniques, Tips, and Best Practices for Scholastic / Collegiate Basketball Officials*. New York: CreateSpace, 2013.

ON THE INTERNET

Becoming an NFL Referee
usatoday30.usatoday.com/sports/nfl/story/2012/09/19/path-to-becoming-nfl-referee-is-usually-long/57809626/1

How to Become a MLB Umpire
mlb.mlb.com/mlb/official_info/umpires/how_to_become.jsp

How to Become a USTA Tennis Official
www.usta.com/About-USTA/Officials/GettingStartedasaUSTAOfficial

NBA Officials
www.nbaofficials.com

USA Hockey Officials
www.usahockey.com/Template_Usahockey.aspx?NAV=OF&ID=19976

USA Volleyball Official Training & Education
www.volleyballreftraining.com

Bibliography

Borden, Sam. "Whistling His Own Tune." *New York Times* online. May 5, 2012. http://www.nytimes.com/2012/05/06/sports/basketball/joey-crawford-sounds-off-on-35-years-as-an-nba-referee.html?_r=5&partner=rss&emc=rss&pagewanted=all& (accessed November 10, 2012).

Borow, Zev. "Tough or Arrogant? Right or Wrong? No Matter What You Think of Umpires, a Week on the Road with Them Proves That They Go Above and Beyond the Call." *ESPN/Magazine*. July 10, 2012. http://sports.espn.go.com/espn/magazine/archives/news/story?page=magazine-20060814-article20 (accessed November 7, 2012).

Clayton, John. "Refereeing can often be full-time job." ESPN.com. September 5, 2012. http://static.espn.go.com/nfl/columns/clayton_john/1248329.html (accessed November 10, 2012).

Education Portal. "How to Become a Certified Baseball Umpire: Career Roadmap." http://education-portal.com/articles/How_to_Become_a_Certified_Baseball_Umpire_Career_Roadmap.html (accessed January 17, 2013).

Giang, Vivian. "The 40 Highest Paying Jobs You Can Get Without a Bachelor's Degree." *Business Insider*. August 7, 2012. http://www.

businessinsider.com/the-40-highest-paying-jobs-you-can-get-without-a-bachelors-degree-2012-8?op=1 (accessed November 7, 2012).

Glier, Ray. "The Life of a Referee." *New York Times* College Sports Blog. November 11, 2012. http://thequad.blogs.nytimes.com/2009/03/29/the-life-of-a-referee (accessed November 11, 2012).

NBA Officials Camp. http://nbaofficials.com (accessed November 11, 2012).

Pawlyna, Andrea. "One Umpire Calls Him Baseball's 'Son of Sam' but Earl Weaver Is Also the Game's Best Manager." *People Magazine* archives online. October 8, 1979. http://www.people.com/people/archive/article/0,,20074761,00.html (accessed November 9, 2012).

Profootballreferee.com. "Has Anyone Ever Lent You a Helping Hand?" http://www.profootballreferee.com/tag/personality-traits (accessed November 8, 2012).

Refstripes.com. "Getting Started in Officiating." http://www.refstripes.com/startofficiating.html (accessed January 18, 2013).

Trex, Ethan. "Umpires and Referees Get Paid What?" *CNNLiving*. October 29, 2009. http://www.cnn.com/2009/LIVING/worklife/10/29/mf.what.umps.get.paid/index.html (accessed November 13, 2012).

Tribou, Doug. "NFL Referees: A Week in the Life." Only a Game. September 8, 2012. http://onlyagame.wbur.org/2012/09/08/nfl-refs-workload (accessed November 8, 2012).

U.S. Bureau of Labor Statistics. "Umpires, Referees, and Other Sports Officials." http://www.bls.gov/ooh/entertainment-and-sports/umpires-referees-and-other-sports-officials.htm (accessed November 7, 2012).

Velasco, Schuyler. "How to Become an NFL Referee? Start Early." *Christian Science Monitor* online. October 29, 2012. http://www.csmonitor.com/Business/2012/1029/How-to-become-an-NFL-referee-Start-early (accessed November 14, 2012).

Index

About the Author

Marty Gitlin is a freelance sportswriter and educational bookwriter based in Cleveland. He has had more than 70 books published. He won more than 45 writing awards as a newspaper sportswriter, including first place for general excellence from the Associated Press.

Picture Credits